Sam Waterston and Robert Prosky in a scene from the New York production of "A Walk in the Woods." Setting designed by Bill Clarke.

A WALK IN THE WOODS

A PLAY IN TWO ACTS
BY LEE BLESSING

DRAMATISTS
PLAY SERVICE
INC.

SPECIAL NOTE

SPECIAL MUSIC TAPE

A WALK IN THE WOODS was presented by Lucille Lortel in association with American Playhouse Theatre Productions and Yale Repertory Theatre at the Booth Theatre in New York City on February 28, 1988. It was directed by Des McAnuff; the setting was designed by Bill Clarke; the costumes were designed by Ellen V. McCartney; the lighting was designed by Richard Riddell; the music was by Michael S. Roth; the sound was designed by G. Thomas Clark; the casting was by Meg Simon/Fran Kumin; and the production stage manager was Maureen F. Gibson. The cast, in order of speaking, was as follows:

ANDREY BOTVINNIK. . . . . .Robert Prosky
JOHN HONEYMAN. . . . . .Sam Waterston

The world premiere of A WALK IN THE WOODS was presented at Yale Repertory Theatre, Lloyd Richards, Artistic Director, Benjamin Mordecai, Managing Director on February 20, 1987. The director was Des McAnuff; set design was by Bill Clarke; lighting design by Jennifer Tipton; costume design by Ellen V. McCartney; music by Michael S. Roth; sound by G. Thomas Clark; production stage manager was Maureen F. Gibson. The cast:

ANDREY BOTVINNIK . . . . .Josef Sommer
JOHN HONEYMAN . . . . .Kenneth Welsh

A WALK IN THE WOODS received its west-coast premiere at the La Jolla Playhouse, Des McAnuff, Artistic Director, Alan Levey, Managing Director on July 14, 1987. The director was Des McAnuff; set design was by Bill Clarke; lighting design by Richard Riddell; costume design by Ellen V. McCartney; music by Michael S. Roth; sound by G. Thomas Clark; production stage manager was Maureen F. Gibson. The cast:

ANDREY BOTVINNIK . . . . Michael Constantine
JOHN HONEYMAN . . . . Lawrence Pressman

A WALK IN THE WOODS was presented as a staged reading at the Eugene O'Neill Theatre Center's 1986 National Playwrights Conference.

CHARACTERS

ANDREY BOTVINNIK. . . . 57, a career Soviet diplomat
JOHN HONEYMAN. . . . . . . 45, an American negotiator

A pleasant woods on the outskirts of Geneva.

To Jeanne Blake
and to Des McAnuff

4

A WALK IN
THE WOODS

ACT ONE

SCENE ONE

A mountain slope on the outskirts of Geneva. Late summer. A sunny morning. The path is well kept, but rustic. It leads to a wooden bench in a little clearing. The overall effect is light, airy, idyllic.
Botvinnik and Honeyman enter. They wear suits—conservative but stylish.

BOTVINNIK. (*With a very slight accent.*) . . . So I told him —this was your reporter, you understand, a network reporter—I told him when Brezhnev was in power, he always began Politburo meetings by saying, "The survival of the Soviet Union depends on the total annihilation of America."

HONEYMAN. (*With a smile.*) You told him *that*?

BOTVINNIK. How was I to know he'd believe it? He actually filed that report with his network. It was nearly broadcast. But, finally someone had the sense to ask him, "Who told you that? Andrey Botvinnik?" (*Laughs slightly.*) And they cancelled it. They know I make jokes. That reporter now I think is covering restaurants. (*Looks around.*) Do you like this place? Shall we sit?

HONEYMAN. Do you think we should stop?

BOTVINNIK. Why not?

HONEYMAN. Well . . . we spoke of this as a walk in the woods.

BOTVINNIK. We are walking, we are sitting, we are walking again . . .

HONEYMAN. But the reporters . . .

BOTVINNIK. Reporters expect us when they see us. They

5

love for us not to be on time. Much speculation. More column inches. (*Pats the bench.*) Come. Sit down.

HONEYMAN. All right. (*They sit.*)

BOTVINNIK. Fine, fine, fine. Now we are sitting. This is good. (*A pause. They stare at the trees.*) The trees are lovely in the late summer here. So full. You came at a good time.

HONEYMAN. It's beautiful.

BOTVINNIK. Have you been to Switzerland before?

HONEYMAN. No.

BOTVINNIK. Well, you must enjoy the lake, the mountain trails and . . . so on and so forth.

HONEYMAN. I will. Thank you.

BOTVINNIK. Mr. McIntyre loved the trails. He was very fond of hiking.

HONEYMAN. Yes, I know.

BOTVINNIK. He told you?

HONEYMAN. Yes.

BOTVINNIK. How is he doing, Mr. McIntyre?

HONEYMAN. Very well. He's with a law firm now in New York.

BOTVINNIK. Really? He's not back at the Arms Control Agency?

HONEYMAN. No. He . . . thought he'd try the private sector again.

BOTVINNIK. (*With sudden enthusiasm, poking Honeyman lightly in the ribs.*) Ah — the private sector! Wonderful thing you Americans have. To think — a refuge from government service. (*Botvinnik stares out at the woods, smiling, Honeyman regards him with surprise.*) Ah, McIntyre. They come and they go, eh?

HONEYMAN. Does that bother you?

BOTVINNIK. (*Smiling.*) Not when someone as pleasant as you is sent to replace him.

HONEYMAN. Thank you very much.

BOTVINNIK. You are very welcome.

HONEYMAN. (*Smiling.*) We're beginning to sound like a pair of diplomats.

BOTVINNIK. We are a pair of diplomats.

HONEYMAN. Well — negotiators.

BOTVINNIK. And negotiators, of course.

6

HONEYMAN. I mean, that is our primary function.

BOTVINNIK. Yes.

HONEYMAN. Diplomacy comes second, in a sense. It's really someone else's job.

BOTVINNIK. If you insist.

HONEYMAN. I don't insist. I'm just trying to be clear, that's all.

BOTVINNIK. You are clear. (*A beat.*)

HONEYMAN. Tell me — why have we taken a walk in the woods?

BOTVINNIK. What do you mean?

HONEYMAN. I mean why. Does your government have something to communicate to us about our new proposal, or . . . ?

BOTVINNIK. No, no, no, no — nothing like that. There are many ways to discuss a proposal. We don't have to come out here.

HONEYMAN. It's a very good proposal.

BOTVINNIK. I know it is.

HONEYMAN. Very good.

BOTVINNIK. Absolutely. On my side, we are all in disarray, believe me. But that's not why we're here. Today, I only want you to see the woods.

HONEYMAN. To see the woods?

BOTVINNIK. Yes. And talk. Simply. Man to man. *Muschina s muschinoi. Da?*

HONEYMAN. Man to man.

BOTVINNIK. The woods are very useful. For months we will be trading proposals across a table. Here, there is no table. We can relax, ignore things. Talk about trees, lakes, whatever.

HONEYMAN. I see. (*A beat.*) The reporters'll be disappointed.

BOTVINNIK. Why?

HONEYMAN. They think we're out here getting all the real work done. (*Botvinnik gives a short, good-natured laugh. A beat.*) So . . . you're not interested in doing any work out here.

BOTVINNIK. What do you call work? Only what we do at the table? This is valuable too.

7

HONEYMAN. What? Sunning ourselves on a bench?

BOTVINNIK. (*Studying him.*) Tell me — do you plan to be a very formal negotiator?

HONEYMAN. Should I be?

BOTVINNIK. *No* — please. Anything but formal. It was the one thing I didn't like about McIntyre. We negotiated for two years, and he never changed his position.

HONEYMAN. The American position changed . . .

BOTVINNIK. No, no — *his* position. Sitting there, at the table. He always sat straight up. For two years he never relaxed. He felt it gave him a moral advantage. It didn't. He looked like a dog waiting for his supper.

HONEYMAN. (*Smiling.*) I'll tell him that.

BOTVINNIK. Would you? It's the one thing I think he should change. Formality allows many things, but it does not allow friendship.

HONEYMAN. I think formality . . .

BOTVINNIK. Formality is simply anger with its hair combed. I could never make a friend out of McIntyre. It was a great disappointment. Two years he sat there: one meter away. Over a hundred sessions. We never became friends. After all, what does that say about me?

HONEYMAN. Is it good, do you think, for arms negotiators to become friends?

BOTVINNIK. Someone has to.

HONEYMAN. But is that, strictly speaking, our job? (*Botvinnik regards Honeyman, then looks away.*)

BOTVINNIK. Perhaps it isn't. (*A beat.*) You'll like the trees here. They are very neutral.

HONEYMAN. (*More concessional.*) I'm only saying, perhaps two disinterested and . . . more formal parties can do a better job negotiating . . .

BOTVINNIK. Tell me — what do you think of the nose on the face of the Reuters correspondent?

HONEYMAN. The Reuters . . . ? Why do you . . . ?

BOTVINNIK. Quick! What do you think?

HONEYMAN. It's very large.

BOTVINNIK. It is *enormous*! I can't look at anything else in press conferences. You wait. You'll stare like I do.

HONEYMAN. Mr. Botvinnik . . .

8

BOTVINNIK. Oh, please — Andrey.

HONEYMAN. Andrey . . .

BOTVINNIK. Andryushka, if you like. Perhaps I could call you Johnny?

HONEYMAN. John would be fine. Andrey, I appreciate your desire to become friends. Indeed, in many of my former negotiations I did become friends with those on the other side. *After* a successful settlement, not before.

BOTVINNIK. I see.

HONEYMAN. I think it's important for us both to remember that there *are* issues here.

BOTVINNIK. Of course.

HONEYMAN. Which must be resolved.

BOTVINNIK. Certainly.

HONEYMAN. Making friends is a fine thing, but not on someone else's time, so to speak. Do you follow me?

BOTVINNIK. Oh, yes.

HONEYMAN. When I took this post, it was to bring something new here. A new formula. A breakthrough.

BOTVINNIK. Yes, yes. A break*through.*

HONEYMAN. A plan I personally helped develop for more than a year.

BOTVINNIK. Wonderful! Welcome! A new man with a new plan. (*Honeyman stares a moment at him.*)

HONEYMAN. I didn't have to come here, you know. I could've stayed safe behind my desk in Washington. Someone more like McIntyre could've been chosen. But, since I have a firsthand knowledge of this proposal, and since I myself have a strong record as a negotiator . . .

BOTVINNIK. At a lower level.

HONEYMAN. . . . at a lower level, I have been asked to work this one through. I have a lot to offer, Andrey. I know these issues. They haven't just sent me to enunciate policy. I'm here to get something done. I hope you'll want to help me.

BOTVINNIK. Whatever I can contribute to the spirit of things . . .

HONEYMAN. I don't want the *spirit* of an agreement. I want an agreement. An honest one — fair to both sides.

BOTVINNIK. I see. Well, who knows? As friends we will certainly . . .
HONEYMAN. No, no — listen.
BOTVINNIK. Yes?
HONEYMAN. What I'm saying about friendship is that it takes us away from the central point.
BOTVINNIK. Which is?
HONEYMAN. Commitment. Mutual commitment to the hard work of negotiating a treaty. We need to find our rewards *there* — in difficult problems, worked on together and solved together. That's the sort of personal relationship I'm seeking here. That's what I would like. (*A beat.*) Andrey? How do you feel about what I'm saying?
BOTVINNIK. Well . . .
HONEYMAN. I'd really like to know.
BOTVINNIK. Would you?
HONEYMAN. Very much.
BOTVINNIK. Very well. I feel . . . (*He leans close to Honeyman.*)
HONEYMAN. Yes?
BOTVINNIK. You have a string on your suit.
HONEYMAN. A string? A thread, you mean?
BOTVINNIK. A thread, yes. Here. (*Botvinnik plucks it off.*) So. Now you look fine. What shall we talk about?
HONEYMAN. You're changing the subject.
BOTVINNIK. I am?
HONEYMAN. Yes.
BOTVINNIK. Really? I'm sorry. What was it please?
HONEYMAN. I was told you like changing the subject.
BOTVINNIK. Not at all. That's a very nice suit, by the way.
HONEYMAN. Mr. McIntyre said it's your favorite ploy.
BOTVINNIK. I never use ploys. Is it Italian?
HONEYMAN. English.
BOTVINNIK. Really? Everything I have is Italian.
HONEYMAN. Are we done talking about this now?
BOTVINNIK. About what?
HONEYMAN. About suits.
BOTVINNIK. If you like.
HONEYMAN. Yes, I do like. Thank you. (*A beat.*) So, will you answer my question.

BOTVINNIK. What question?

HONEYMAN. My question about whether or not you agree that we shouldn't be friends.

BOTVINNIK. Was that the subject? Before? That I changed?

HONEYMAN. Yes, it was.

BOTVINNIK. Ah. Well, my answer is of course that I agree with you.

HONEYMAN. You agree?

BOTVINNIK. Yes.

HONEYMAN. That we shouldn't be friends?

BOTVINNIK. Yes.

HONEYMAN. That's not what you said before.

BOTVINNIK. But then I didn't know your view. Now I do, and I want to agree with you.

HONEYMAN. You want to agree with me.

BOTVINNIK. Yes.

HONEYMAN. Why?

BOTVINNIK. Because you are my friend.

HONEYMAN. I can't be your friend. That's my whole position.

BOTVINNIK. Yes. And I agree.

HONEYMAN. You can't agree.

BOTVINNIK. But I do.

HONEYMAN. You're contradicting yourself.

BOTVINNIK. I know. But I will go to any length to keep a friend. (*A beat. They stare at each other.*)

HONEYMAN. I was told you liked to contradict yourself.

BOTVINNIK. Will you pardon me a moment? (*Botvinnik takes out a small, plastic eyedropper, places drops in his eyes.*)

HONEYMAN. Is something wrong with your eyes?

BOTVINNIK. Hm? No, no. They become very dry, that's all. It is most uncomfortable. I'm sorry.

HONEYMAN. Are you seeing a doctor?

BOTVINNIK. Several of them. Over the last month or two. Swiss doctors. It is nothing.

HONEYMAN. What do they say?

BOTVINNIK. Do you want this for your files?

HONEYMAN. I was only . . .

BOTVINNIK. I will tell you. They tell me I have Sjogren's syndrome.

11

HONEYMAN. Sjogren's syndrome? What's that mean?

BOTVINNIK. It means I have dry eyes.

HONEYMAN. That's all?

BOTVINNIK. That's all. Dry eyes, dry nose, dry mouth. Whatever should be wet is dry.

HONEYMAN. What can they do for it?

BOTVINNIK. Nothing. They told me to eat wet food. They gave me artificial tears. "Live with it," they said. "Klee did."

HONEYMAN. Klee?

BOTVINNIK. Paul Klee. The Swiss artist. He too, apparently, had this problem. The doctors took great pride in telling me. Imagine — having national pride in a disease. (*Putting the eyedrops away.*) I'm sorry for the delay. That was not a ploy, however — only a sickness. What were we discussing?

HONEYMAN. Perhaps we should be getting back. If you don't feel well . . .

BOTVINNIK. No, no, no — I'm fine.

HONEYMAN. Still, it's probably time.

BOTVINNIK. We just got here. Don't you like it?

HONEYMAN. I like it fine. It's just that I'd prefer . . .

BOTVINNIK. A table. Yes, I know.

HONEYMAN. No, not a table. What's said over it. I need some seriousness. I think we owe our governments that much, don't you?

BOTVINNIK. Do you like me?

HONEYMAN. Andrey . . .

BOTVINNIK. Answer my question.

HONEYMAN. I'm not going to answer your question, I'm going back now. (*He starts out.*)

BOTVINNIK. Without me? (*Honeyman hesitates.*) What would the reporters think of that? We leave together, return separately? Significant rumors. (*Honeyman stares at Botvinnik, returns.*) So tell me — aren't you embarrassed to be an American?

HONEYMAN. No.

BOTVINNIK. I am. To be Russian, I mean.

HONEYMAN. Why?

BOTVINNIK. Look at us: Americans and Russians. The world's great powers — the world's great fools. Year after year we sit here, among the mountaintops. We talk about our weapons — so many of them. Weapons on land, in the sea, in the air, in space. Too many. "Let's get rid of some," we say, "before there's an accident." We talk *so* seriously, we calculate, we make proposals. And we nearly always fail. It's embarrassing. The best we can do is take away a few missiles once in awhile for show. Beyond that, nothing. If the world was not terrified of us, it would laugh.

HONEYMAN. That may be, but . . .

BOTVINNIK. Why are we failing? I ask myself this. For years we have been here. We keep failing.

HONEYMAN. I think the reasons are . . .

BOTVINNIK. (*With sudden conviction.*) I know the reason! I have finally discovered who is to blame. Would you like to know?

HONEYMAN. Andrey . . .

BOTVINNIK. It is not America. It is not the Soviet Union. Ask me who is to blame.

HONEYMAN. *Andrey* . . .

BOTVINNIK. Ask me. (*A beat.*)

HONEYMAN. Who, Andrey? Who is to blame?

BOTVINNIK. Switzerland.

HONEYMAN. I'm going.

BOTVINNIK. No, John — listen. Let me explain. Then we can go.

HONEYMAN. You're being ridiculous.

BOTVINNIK. Not if you listen. Switzerland has two things only: mountains and peace. Thousands of mountains, centuries of peace. Peaceful trees, peaceful lakes, peaceful people. You can't invade it — too many mountains. Besides, there's nothing here. Only trees and Swiss people. So, what does mankind use Switzerland for? Peace conferences.

HONEYMAN. Andrey.

BOTVINNIK. But what happens? We sit across the table and look very grave, and talk and debate and argue about imminent world destruction. Then we leave the table, go outside, and what do we see? Rich, happy, *peaceful* people. Unharmed buildings, no barricades, no rifles, not even littering. We breathe air that hasn't known a war in centuries. Suddenly, things look better. Why agree to a treaty now?

We'll wait. I tell you, my friend, the real problem is Switzerland itself.

HONEYMAN. Do you always joke about these matters?

BOTVINNIK. Who is joking? We should put the table at the bottom of a missile silo. Then we would negotiate. I have seriously suggested this to my superiors.

HONEYMAN. And what did they say?

BOTVINNIK. They said to stop joking. (*A beat.*)

HONEYMAN. May I ask you a personal question?

BOTVINNIK. Of course.

HONEYMAN. Why, in heaven's name, haven't you been replaced? (*Botvinnik laughs.*)

BOTVINNIK. Mr. McIntyre also asked me this question.

HONEYMAN. What's the answer?

BOTVINNIK. (*After a slight hesitation, smiling.*) You have done your research, I presume. Perhaps you should tell me. (*A beat.*)

HONEYMAN. You're a very good negotiator. That's why they keep you. You can say "no" longer than other people. You can say it with a frown, you can say it with a smile. You can say no and still be so charming, we'll think you said yes. You dress well, you speak English well, you're good with the media. Most of all, you know how to take orders — at least when it really counts. And the orders are nearly always the same: say no, and look good doing it. They keep you here because you give them something special. Not just a man who says no, but a personality.

BOTVINNIK. Is that how I am seen? How very flattering.

HONEYMAN. I've done other research. Want to hear?

BOTVINNIK. Certainly. I love to hear about me.

HONEYMAN. In your private conversations you are . . . less dependable. It's believed your leaders worry quite a bit over your congeniality towards Westerners. You have a penchant for changing the subject, you contradict yourself, you deliberately misunderstand things. Your behavior is sometimes seen as childish.

BOTVINNIK. Childish?

HONEYMAN. Mr. McIntyre wasn't sure if you were in complete control of these conversational gambits. He wondered if they weren't genuine liabilities that would grow

14

worse with time, and destroy your effectiveness. But do you know what I think? You know what my personal opinion is?

BOTVINNIK. What?

HONEYMAN. That you are in full control of what you're doing, both formally and informally. That the very word effectiveness in your mind means obstruction. That you—and perhaps your country—are fundamentally dedicated to *not* finding a significant agreement.

BOTVINNIK. You are very blunt. But, this is refreshing. Please—go on. You're doing so well.

HONEYMAN. I'm not the only one in my country with this opinion. The fact is, I was appointed for this job precisely because it was thought only someone of my special talents could work with you at all.

BOTVINNIK. Special talents? Yes, I must admit, we were very impressed when you were chosen: a man with no experience in Geneva . . .

HONEYMAN. I had experience elsewhere.

BOTVINNIK. At a lower level.

HONEYMAN. *And* was effective.

BOTVINNIK. A man who speaks only English.

HONEYMAN. I speak technical Russian.

BOTVINNIK. No one "speaks" technical Russian. It's like saying "I speak Algebra." A man who . . .

HONEYMAN. You're ignoring one positive.

BOTVINNIK. There's a positive?

HONEYMAN. I'm an extremely effective negotiator. That doesn't mean I say no well. It means I say yes well. At the right time. When the right work has been done. When I negotiate, I find an agreement.

BOTVINNIK. So you think we will agree, eh? Eventually?

HONEYMAN. Yes. We will.

BOTVINNIK. Perhaps you are right. But tell me something—even if we do agree, do you think it will matter? (*Rising, taking a deep breath, exhaling briskly.*) Do you like the mountain air? I don't. I come from Leningrad. Sea air. That is air you can feel—it has weight. This air is too thin, too sterile.

HONEYMAN. Too healthy, you mean.

BOTVINNIK. Only oxygen. It's not enough. You know, I

15

have breathed the air in many places . . .

HONEYMAN. (*Rising.*) Andrey, I'm not interested in the air you have breathed. I'm interested in creating an agreement. Nothing else. And yes, I do believe it's going to matter. I think you'll be surprised, in fact, how much it does matter. Now, I'm going to go back. Not because I feel defeated, or hopeless. I'm going back because I feel we've done as much as we can do today, and tomorrow — over a table — we'll do more. And I'm going whether you come along or not.

BOTVINNIK. I would love to go now. I'm glad you have suggested it. (*Honeyman stops, turns back.*)

HONEYMAN. Do we understand each other?

BOTVINNIK. What do you mean?

HONEYMAN. Do we understand each other? I want to feel this conversation has served a purpose.

BOTVINNIK. Really? Why?

HONEYMAN. Because all conversations should.

BOTVINNIK. They should?

HONEYMAN. Yes, they should. Do we understand each other?

BOTVINNIK. Of course we do. We are friends.

HONEYMAN. No, we are not friends.

BOTVINNIK. We're becoming friends.

HONEYMAN. We're not becoming friends.

BOTVINNIK. Of course we are.

HONEYMAN. Andrey, we've just . . . Do you know what they call you? In the American Delegation? The Crab. Not because you're mean or irritable. Because you never go in a straight line.

BOTVINNIK. (*Pointing at Honeyman's shoes.*) Are those Italian shoes?

HONEYMAN. Don't talk about my shoes.

BOTVINNIK. They are Italian.

HONEYMAN. They're French . . .

BOTVINNIK. French shoes?! Who would buy French shoes? I can get you good Italian . . .

HONEYMAN. I'm happy with the shoes I have, thank you!!

BOTVINNIK. You know, you have great personal charm. You are much warmer than McIntyre.

HONEYMAN. (*With a short, frustrated sigh.*) I am much more persistent than McIntyre. I'm here to make a treaty with you, not a friendship. You can behave as erratically as you like. My offer stands. Work with me. Please.
BOTVINNIK. (*With apparent disapproval.*) Where do you get your ties?
HONEYMAN. (*Starting out.*) I'm going.
BOTVINNIK. (*Following.*) This is wonderful! We are doing so well together. When should we take another walk?
HONEYMAN. (*Stopping.*) Never.
BOTVINNIK. Never? Are you sure, my friend?
HONEYMAN. (*Exiting.*) I'm sure!
BOTVINNIK. (*Staring at the bench.*) Very well — whatever you say. After all, we are here to agree. (*Honeyman reappears, stares at Botvinnik. Botvinnik gestures graciously and follows him out. Lights fade on the empty clearing.*)

END OF ACT ONE, SCENE ONE

SCENE TWO

The same scene. Noon, two months later. It is fall. Botvinnik sits on the bench. Honeyman paces, speaking heatedly, but not without control. Botvinnik on the other hand, is quite relaxed.

HONEYMAN. . . . and believe me, the State Department is not going to be patient with this. We made this proposal months ago. Since then you've done nothing but argue over details.
BOTVINNIK. We are making a careful examination . . .
HONEYMAN. You're stalling! You're using a tiny point to hold up a major agreement.
BOTVINNIK. Tiny to you . . .
HONEYMAN. Tiny. To anyone. Do you want to know what the President thinks? (*Botvinnik shrugs acquiescently.*) He's called me twice this week. He flew me home last week. "What's wrong with Botvinnik?" he asks, "Has he said no so

17

many times he's forgotten how to say yes?" (*Botvinnik laughs.*) Well? Have you?

BOTVINNIK. You have an amusing President. I hope he does well in the election.

HONEYMAN. Whether he wins or loses will have no effect on our proposal.

BOTVINNIK. (*Brushing leaves off the bench.*) Perhaps. Come, sit down. Relax.

HONEYMAN. You're purposely holding off, aren't you?

BOTVINNIK. Well . . .

HONEYMAN. The more time you waste trying for a slight advantage from our elections, the colder this proposal gets.

BOTVINNIK. So don't have so many elections. Look how bright the leaves are! I'm glad you asked me to take this walk. You said we would never do it again, but here we are.

HONEYMAN. You're not going to exploit our political process.

BOTVINNIK. Your political process exploits itself. So does ours. How does your side act when our leaders are old and sick? Do you rush into negotiations? No, you wait. You *should* wait.

HONEYMAN. So when do we negotiate agreements? When there isn't a president up for election? When there isn't a Soviet leader in bad health? How often is that?

BOTVINNIK. Now and then.

HONEYMAN. Now and then? You want to discuss the life or death of this planet *now and then*?

BOTVINNIK. You think it should be more often?

HONEYMAN. Andrey, this is our best proposal to date. The President's dedicated himself to the image of a peacemaker. He wants to do some lasting work. You should take advantage of that.

BOTVINNIK. I'm as sorry for the delay as you. But you must understand. Our leaders are naturally careful. The experience of the war for us was . . .

HONEYMAN. That was forty years ago!

BOTVINNIK. But still . . .

HONEYMAN. But nothing. It's a dead issue. Your country has made a state religion out of what's essentially smugness.

"No one suffered the way we suffered. Twenty million died."

BOTVINNIK. Twenty million did die.

HONEYMAN. Eighty million died. All over the world. Everybody suffered. The Soviet government has no more right than anyone else to preach absolutes because of it.

BOTVINNIK. This is marvelous. I was pleased when you suggested a walk, but to find such emotion. This is very wonderful. Thank you.

HONEYMAN. Don't digress.

BOTVINNIK. I'm sorry.

HONEYMAN. My point is, any past horror, any breakdown of civilization can be used for decades thereafter by an unscrupulous government to frighten a population into impotence and obedience.

BOTVINNIK. And that is what we have done?

HONEYMAN. Yes. It is. (*Botvinnik smiles, uninsulted.*) Aren't you going to disagree?

BOTVINNIK. Maybe later. Go on—please.

HONEYMAN. So . . . anyway, I feel the excuse that your leaders are overcautious because of the experience of World War II is a cynical, self-serving and manipulative . . . lie. An outdated lie at that. (*His tone has grown softer before Botvinnik's open, unoffended gaze.*) And I wish you wouldn't do it anymore.

BOTVINNIK. Very well. In our private conversation, I will not speak of it again.

HONEYMAN. Well . . . fine. Thank you.

BOTVINNIK. Don't mention it.

HONEYMAN. You know, I don't think your government appreciates the . . .

BOTVINNIK. (*Holding up a bright yellow leaf.*) Tell me, what kind of leaf is this?

HONEYMAN. Andrey . . .

BOTVINNIK. Just what kind? Please.

HONEYMAN. That's a linden.

BOTVINNIK. Linden. Very nice. Botany—that's your hobby. I remember from our reports on you. (*Twirling the leaf.*) Yellow as sunlight, eh? Do you have these in Wisconsin?

HONEYMAN. (*Sighing.*) Yes. We call it basswood.

BOTVINNIK. Basswood? Like the fish?

HONEYMAN. I don't know. Andrey, I may have been a little harsh just now, but . . .

BOTVINNIK. It is my great regret I have never visited your country.

HONEYMAN. Thank you. All I was trying to say was . . .

BOTVINNIK. Your home city. What is it—Wausau? (*This he pronounces poorly—something like: Vah-sow.*)

HONEYMAN. Wausau.

BOTVINNIK. (*Nodding, as though their pronunciations match.*) Vah-sow.

HONEYMAN. No. No, Wau-sau. Wausau, Wisconsin. Andrey, if I was harsh, it's only because . . .

BOTVINNIK. (*Practicing it, but no better.*) Vah-sow.

HONEYMAN. Andrey . . .

BOTVINNIK. I think I have it now: Vah-sow.

HONEYMAN. (*Angrily.*) Wausau! It's Wausau! You can say it, you speak English perfectly!

BOTVINNIK. I'm only trying to . . .

HONEYMAN. You're only trying to irritate me! I can see that! But why!? Do you feel it gives you the upper hand? It doesn't. If these talks fail, we both look bad. You realize that, don't you?

BOTVINNIK. I have failed before.

HONEYMAN. I haven't. (*A beat.*) What about this tiny point? When can we expect movement from your side?

BOTVINNIK. After your election.

HONEYMAN. That's five weeks from now.

BOTVINNIK. We can only go so fast. We have hawks and doves, just like you. Sometimes the hawks eat a few doves.

HONEYMAN. This is ludicrous. The President won't accept this.

BOTVINNIK. He'll have no choice.

HONEYMAN. What if we force the matter?

BOTVINNIK. You could lose the whole proposal.

HONEYMAN. Of course you have to say that.

BOTVINNIK. (*With a tone of complete frankness.*) You'll lose the proposal. (*Honeyman walks away from Botvinnik, kicks at the ground angrily.*) A frustrating business, yes?

HONEYMAN. Quiet, please.

BOTVINNIK. You're upset. Perhaps you would like to be alone. I can go back now. Excuse me. (*Botvinnik starts out.*)

HONEYMAN. Andrey.

BOTVINNIK. Yes?

HONEYMAN. If we go back so soon the reporters might think we're in trouble on this.

BOTVINNIK. We are in trouble on this.

HONEYMAN. There's no reason for *them* to think so.

BOTVINNIK. I thought you believed in freedom of the press.

HONEYMAN. Don't be cute. Come back and sit down.

BOTVINNIK. (*Returning to the bench.*) What shall we talk about?

HONEYMAN. We don't have to talk about anything. We just have to wait here a decent amount of time.

BOTVINNIK. Ah. (*Honeyman sits beside him. The two men stare out in different directions for a long moment.*) How are we doing?

HONEYMAN. You could use your influence, you know. They listen to you about these things.

BOTVINNIK. Not always.

HONEYMAN. Sometimes. So why not talk to them?

BOTVINNIK. It can be risky. It could put me out of fashion with the leadership.

HONEYMAN. Out of fashion?

BOTVINNIK. It's not an insignificant risk. (*A beat.*)

HONEYMAN. Could anything induce you to take that risk?

BOTVINNIK. (*His face lighting up expectantly.*) Is this a bribe?

HONEYMAN. No.

BOTVINNIK. Too bad. I never accept bribes, but I love to know what's being offered.

HONEYMAN. I mean, is there anything we can do to convince you to help? That's all I mean.

BOTVINNIK. What can the Americans do? To make me want to take chances with my career?

HONEYMAN. Yes.

BOTVINNIK. Absolutely nothing. (*Honeyman gives a short sigh of frustration.*) Now ask me what you can do.

HONEYMAN. You just said. We can't . . .

BOTVINNIK. No, no—you. John Honeyman. What can you do to get me to help. Ask me that. (*Honeyman eyes him distrustfully.*)

HONEYMAN. What . . . um, what is there I can do?

BOTVINNIK. Are you sure you want to know?

HONEYMAN. Yes, I want to know.

BOTVINNIK. Are you completely sure?

HONEYMAN. *Tell me.* What can I do?

BOTVINNIK. (*Almost conspiratorial.*) Be frivolous with me.

HONEYMAN. Frivolous?

BOTVINNIK. Yes. Frivolous. (*A beat.*)

HONEYMAN. What does . . . frivolous mean?

BOTVINNIK. It's your language.

HONEYMAN. I know . . .

BOTVINNIK. Don't you know the word?

HONEYMAN. Of course I know the word. It's just that . . .

BOTVINNIK. (*Finishing his sentence for him.*) A word may have many meanings.

HONEYMAN. Exactly.

BOTVINNIK. What do you think I mean? By frivolous. Do you think I mean playful? Impractical? (*Honeyman stares at him cautiously.*) Irrelevant? Unimportant? Superficial? (*A beat.*) With unbecoming levity? (*Honeyman rises, moves off a step or two.*) I am sorry. To me, frivolous means not serious.

HONEYMAN. Not serious? That's all? Just . . . not serious?

BOTVINNIK. That's all.

HONEYMAN. You want to have a . . . frivolous conversation? (*Botvinnik smiles.*) And for that you'd be willing to try and influence your superiors? If I gave you that? (*Botvinnik nods.*) Why?

BOTVINNIK. Nothing else is interesting to me. Whenever I speak with Americans, they always ask. "What about war? What about Afghanistan? What about cruise missiles?" It is no longer interesting to me.

HONEYMAN. But what about cruise missiles? (*Botvinnik instantly holds up a hand in a silencing gesture.*) Sorry.

22

BOTVINNIK. I hear certain words—whether I say them or someone else says them—words like "detente," "human rights," "Star Wars," "Central America," "readiness," "early warning," and I feel like I am falling away from the Earth. I can see the Earth—the entire planet, like I am a cosmonaut. And it is falling away from me. We are both simply . . . receding into the dark. Sometimes I spend entire conversations in this kind of darkness, while I am hearing words like "summit," "test ban," "emigration," "strategic objectives." It is almost as though the words are printed . . . on the dark walls . . . all around me. And the Earth is by then like a . . . fingertip, it is so far away. (*A beat.*) Does this ever happen to you?

HONEYMAN. No.

BOTVINNIK. Perhaps it will someday. In any case, you must forgive me. This does not happen at the table. There, I listen very carefully. There, I pretend we are discussing a different planet from Earth, and that helps very much.

HONEYMAN. Andrey . . .

BOTVINNIK. Receptions, dinner parties—that's where it happens. I hear all those serious words: "lasers," "megadeaths," "acceptable losses" . . . Do you know what I am dying to hear an American talk about? Mickey Mouse. Cowboys. How to make a banjo . . .

HONEYMAN. I don't think . . .

BOTVINNIK. Minnie Mouse. Anything that is not serious.

HONEYMAN. I can't talk about Minnie Mouse with you.

BOTVINNIK. But that is my price. For helping you. For doing what I can.

HONEYMAN. You want to be frivolous.

BOTVINNIK. Very much. (*A beat.*)

HONEYMAN. I'm disappointed by this. I thought you were more professional.

BOTVINNIK. This *is* professional. This is how to survive as a professional.

HONEYMAN. (*Regards him skeptically, then with resolve.*) Fine. Let's survive then. Frivolously. What shall we talk about?

BOTVINNIK. Whatever you like.

HONEYMAN. You decide; it's your idea.

BOTVINNIK. Very well, let me see. Do you like Country and Western music?

HONEYMAN. Honestly?

BOTVINNIK. Of course honestly. Why hide anything? We're being frivolous.

HONEYMAN. Yes, I do like it.

BOTVINNIK. Wonderful! So do I. It's very anti-Soviet, but nothing is perfect. (*A beat.*) *Blue Eyes Crying In the Rain*, eh?

HONEYMAN. Yes.

BOTVINNIK. Wonderful song. Very sad. It could have been Russian.

HONEYMAN. Maybe.

BOTVINNIK. Have you ever slept with a redhead?

HONEYMAN. No.

BOTVINNIK. Neither have I. It is a great regret. (*A beat. They stare out.*) You say something.

HONEYMAN. Me?

BOTVINNIK. Yes.

HONEYMAN. What should I say?

BOTVINNIK. Anything. Whatever is on your mind.

HONEYMAN. Right. Well, um . . . sometimes I notice when we're discussing space weapons technology . . .

BOTVINNIK. *No!* No, no, no, no, no!

HONEYMAN. I only meant *when* we're discussing space weapons . . .

BOTVINNIK. No! You are too serious.

HONEYMAN. Even to mention it? On the way to something else?

BOTVINNIK. *Too serious!* (*A beat. Botvinnik's look is fierce.*)

HONEYMAN. I'm sorry.

BOTVINNIK. No problem. Try again. Be trivial.

HONEYMAN. Well . . . let's see. OK, um — I hate brown suits.

BOTVINNIK. And?

HONEYMAN. And what?

BOTVINNIK. You hate brown suits, and . . . ?

HONEYMAN. And nothing. I hate brown suits — that's all. (*Botvinnik is disappointed. He rises, walks away towards the edge of the trees.*) What's wrong? Isn't that trivial enough?

BOTVINNIK. There's a difference between trivial and boring.

HONEYMAN. That's not boring.

BOTVINNIK. Of course it is. (*Mimicking Honeyman.*) "I hate brown suits . . ."?

HONEYMAN. It's no more boring than your liking Willie Nelson.

BOTVINNIK. It is.

HONEYMAN. It is not.

BOTVINNIK. You are just not good at this. Admit it.

HONEYMAN. I can be as trivial as the next person. You never said I had to be trivial and entertaining at the same time.

BOTVINNIK. It goes without saying.

HONEYMAN. It does not.

BOTVINNIK. Now you are just arguing with me.

HONEYMAN. I'm not arguing.

BOTVINNIK. You are.

HONEYMAN. *Kindly stop telling me what I am and am not doing!* (*Botvinnik is delighted.*)

BOTVINNIK. That was very good. Tell me another trivial thing.

HONEYMAN. I can't.

BOTVINNIK. Of course you can. You must, if we are to have any fun.

HONEYMAN. *I* am not having fun.

BOTVINNIK. Be patient. If you stay here long enough, the only thing you'll be able to enjoy is a totally meaningless conversation.

HONEYMAN. Have you failed that much here? (*A beat.*) I'm sorry. I can't be frivolous anymore.

BOTVINNIK. (*Throws his hands up in mock despair.*) What can I do? He refuses to humor me. Such a small price, and he will not pay it. I'm beginning to miss Mr. McIntyre. (*Botvinnik takes out his eyedrops.*)

HONEYMAN. All I know is, considering who we are, and where we are, and what we have been sent here to do, it is literally wasting the world's time for us to be anything but deadly serious with each other.

BOTVINNIK. Wasting the world's time. I like that.

HONEYMAN. Don't grade my phrasemaking, talk to me.
BOTVINNIK. Seriously?
HONEYMAN. Seriously.
BOTVINNIK. (*Considering this, then shaking his head.*) Too boring.
HONEYMAN. (*As Botvinnik starts to put the eyedrops away.*) You know, it's a shame those tears of yours can't be real.
BOTVINNIK. (*Dropping the bottle back into his pocket.*) What if I talk seriously to you, and you don't enjoy it?
HONEYMAN. If it's serious, I'll enjoy it.
BOTVINNIK. You will, eh?
HONEYMAN. Yes.
BOTVINNIK. Very well then. (*With a sudden formality.*) I will now present to you my serious thoughts on the subject of . . . let's see . . . the character of the Russian and American people.
HONEYMAN. I don't think that's . . .
BOTVINNIK. That's my topic. It is fundamental. Do you object?
HONEYMAN. Not as long as you're serious.
BOTVINNIK. Deadly. (*A beat. Honeyman nods.*) Good. There is a great difference between Russians and Americans—yes or no?
HONEYMAN. Well . . . yes, if you . . .
BOTVINNIK. There is no difference. I will prove it. If the Russians and not the English had come to America, what would they have done?
HONEYMAN. They would have . . .
BOTVINNIK. They would have killed all the Indians and taken all the land. See? No difference. Americans and Russians are just the same. But their history is different. What is history? History is geography over time. The geography of America is oceans—therefore no nearby enemies. The geography of Russia is the opposite: flat, broad plains—open invitations to anyone who wants to attack. Mongols, French, Germans, Poles, Turks, Swedes—anyone. Do you agree with this? Of course you do—it is obviously true.
HONEYMAN. Andrey . . .
BOTVINNIK. Quiet, I am being serious. So, what is the history of America? Conquest without competition. What is

26

the history of Russia? Conquest *because* of competition. How best to be America? Make individual freedom your god. This allows you to attack on many fronts—all along your borders, in fact—and maintain the illusion that you are not attacking at all. You don't even have to call your wars wars. You call them "settling the west."

HONEYMAN. That's a gross misreading of . . .

BOTVINNIK. Don't interrupt. How best to be Russia then? Fight collectively. *Know* that you are trying to crush those around you. Make control your god, and channel the many wills of the people into one will. Only this will be effective. Only this will defeat your neighbors.

HONEYMAN. I'm leaving now.

BOTVINNIK. You can't. This is what you wanted.

HONEYMAN. I wanted a *conversation*.

BOTVINNIK. (*Pushing on.*) So—what is the result of all this history and geography? Why are the Russians and Americans—people who have done the same thing: create and maintain empires—why are we now enemies to the death?

HONEYMAN. We're not enemies, we're rival . . .

BOTVINNIK. We are enemies! (*A beat. Then softer.*) Because Americans, who never had to confront themselves as conquerors, are still under the delusion that they are idealists. And Russians, who did have to confront themselves, are under the equally powerful delusion that they are realists. I'm speaking now of those in power. Common Americans and common Russians share a much simpler delusion: that they are peace-loving people.

HONEYMAN. This is profoundly cynical.

BOTVINNIK. Thank you. I like to be clear-eyed. (*Quietly.*) You cannot work at this job as long as I have without realizing that no one wants you to succeed. Not even the man on the street.

HONEYMAN. How on earth can you think that?

BOTVINNIK. Go to the street. Ask the man. Ask him, "Do you want to get rid of all nuclear weapons right now?" Of course, he will say yes. Then ask "Are you willing to give up your country's power, prestige and predominance in the world?" He will say no. But the two questions are the same.

27

Without nuclear weapons, our empires would no longer *be* empires. They would simply be countries among other countries.

HONEYMAN. Powerful countries.

BOTVINNIK. But not *super*powers. We are too used to dominating, John. We will never give that up.

HONEYMAN. There are other ways to be superpowers.

BOTVINNIK. Without nuclear weapons, we will be nothing more than a rich, powerful Canada and an enormous Poland. (*A beat.*) There is a more important reason, as well.

HONEYMAN. Which is?

BOTVINNIK. The most exciting thing in the world is to know we can destroy the world. Like that. In a day. To know the bombs and the soldiers are in place. Their hands at the controls. The computers constantly running, monitoring, ready. We have never known such excitement. Alexander, Napoleon, Hitler would give up all of their conquests just to live in a world where such destruction is possible. Man has worked a long time for this. He is an animal who must fulfill every potential. Even the potential to kill himself. Even the potential to kill everything else.

HONEYMAN. It's simpleminded to say just because man *can* kill himself, that that's what he's going to do.

BOTVINNIK. It is? Look at the money, time and energy our governments put into making ready for war. What do we put into making ready for peace? You and me. That's all.

HONEYMAN. Governments have always armed themselves to the teeth, but mankind truly does hate war.

BOTVINNIK. If mankind hated war, there would be millions of us and only two soldiers. (*A beat.*) Is this a serious enough conversation for you? Do you want to go on?

HONEYMAN. Not really.

BOTVINNIK. Perhaps we should go back then. (*Botvinnik starts out.*)

HONEYMAN. Wait.

BOTVINNIK. Yes?

HONEYMAN. What will you do about helping us?

BOTVINNIK. Nothing, of course.

HONEYMAN. Why not? I met your condition. I talked about trivial things . . .

BOTVINNIK. Brown suits? That was pitiful.

HONEYMAN. I'll try again.

BOTVINNIK. You're no good at it. You have no need for it.

HONEYMAN. I'll develop the need.

BOTVINNIK. Over time, yes. But now it only makes you uncomfortable.

HONEYMAN. Help us anyway.

BOTVINNIK. Why should I?

HONEYMAN. For the sake of peace.

BOTVINNIK. What kind of peace? Peace where you dominate? Peace where we dominate?

HONEYMAN. Peace where we share. You say man has to fulfill every potential — that he's that kind of animal. But he has other potentials — not just destructiveness. Andrey, man has the potential to become a whole new animal. One that trusts instead of fears. One that agrees when it makes sense to agree. That finds the way to live, because life has become for him — has *finally* become — a sacred thing.

BOTVINNIK. Only a child could believe this.

HONEYMAN. I believe it.

BOTVINNIK. Good. You will always be young. (*Botvinnik turns to go.*)

HONEYMAN. Andrey! (*Botvinnik stops.*) Do you think it's a virtue to have been here as long as you have? You think cynicism is some sort of glorious end product of your work here? You know, it's just as possible that I'm the one who sees clearly, not you! Precisely because I *haven't* been here — slowly going blind from my failures. (*Softening his tone.*) Andrey, we have no choice. If we don't believe in our ability to save ourselves, then everything dies. Everything. All through history, man has been able to love destruction and be excited by violence — because no matter what stupid, gaping terror he created, it was always *survivable.* But no more. If we fail now, history itself will disappear. Time will stop. There won't be any right way to think or feel, because there won't be anyone here to have thoughts or feelings. There will be no *here.* (*A beat.*) Idealism is no longer a choice for mankind. It's a necessity. We have to find whatever crumbs of pure, good will exist in us. We have to feed whatever tiny inclination we have towards each other. We have to

29

start with the bare fact that there *are* two of us here. *At least.* That underneath whatever motivations bring us here — hate, fear, gain, *whatever* — there is something that will, ultimately, save us.

BOTVINNIK. What?

HONEYMAN. Recognition. We look across the table, and we see ourselves. (*A beat.*) Andrey. Help me. (*Botvinnik sits and removes a small stone from his shoe.*)

BOTVINNIK. Do you know what they think of initiative in my country?

HONEYMAN. Even now? With the new openness?

BOTVINNIK. Please.

HONEYMAN. Your leaders respect your opinion.

BOTVINNIK. Because I keep it to myself.

HONEYMAN. Help me.

BOTVINNIK. No.

HONEYMAN. You owe it to yourself to push your leaders for an agreement.

BOTVINNIK. Ridiculous.

HONEYMAN. It's not ridiculous. I push my leaders constantly. I've been arguing with the administration for weeks. The President is already sorry he appointed me.

BOTVINNIK. So am I. (*A beat.*)

HONEYMAN. The President's considering making our proposal public.

BOTVINNIK. He wouldn't.

HONEYMAN. I've told him not to, but . . .

BOTVINNIK. That would end the proposal.

HONEYMAN. I know.

BOTVINNIK. We would have no choice but to reject it.

HONEYMAN. I know, but that's how strongly he feels. (*A beat.*) Plus, he's worried about the election. He thinks it might enhance his position if he announced our . . . peace efforts.

BOTVINNIK. So this is what from you? A threat?

HONEYMAN. It's not a threat. It's a . . .

BOTVINNIK. Promise?

HONEYMAN. He needs a gesture. From you. Movement on something. Anything. Big, small — it doesn't matter. Something that will give him faith.

30

BOTVINNIK. He needs us to give him faith? Really! (*He starts out.*)
HONEYMAN. I thought you wanted to be my friend.
BOTVINNIK. (*Stopping.*) I am your friend.
HONEYMAN. No, you're not. Not unless you do this for me. I swear, Andrey, if you don't push for this — right now — you and I will never be friends. I'll be stiffer and stuffier than anyone you've ever dealt with. I will out-McIntyre McIntyre.
BOTVINNIK. This is not fair.
HONEYMAN. It's my price. For friendship. Will you pay it? (*A beat. They stare at each other.*)
BOTVINNIK. All right. I will suggest that we not wait for the election. That we treat your proposal more seriously.
HONEYMAN. Thank you.
BOTVINNIK. That's all I will do. Suggest it. Once. Lightly.
HONEYMAN. Thank you very much.
BOTVINNIK. Don't mention it.
HONEYMAN. You know, I think we're beginning to get along.
BOTVINNIK. You do, do you?
HONEYMAN. Yes. I mean, here we are — agreeing on something.
BOTVINNIK. You think you did it all by yourself, eh?
HONEYMAN. Not by myself . . .
BOTVINNIK. John Honeyman — the great convincer. Send him to Switzerland and peace will follow.
HONEYMAN. I didn't mean that.
BOTVINNIK. Yes, you did. But think what you like. I'm helping you for one reason only: it might be entertaining.
HONEYMAN. Entertaining?
BOTVINNIK. But I doubt it. (*Botvinnik turns to go.*)
HONEYMAN. Shall I go with you?
BOTVINNIK. No. Since we are agreeing to do this, we should come back separately. It will confuse the reporters. (*Botvinnik exits. A beat.*)
HONEYMAN. (*Calling out.*) Thank you!
BOTVINNIK. (*Off.*) Don't shout thank you in the woods!
HONEYMAN. (*Calling.*) I'm sorry!
BOTVINNIK. (*Off.*) Don't shout I'm sorry! (*Honeyman draws*

31

in breath to shout something else, then stops. Smiles.)
HONEYMAN. (*In a normal voice.*) Then I won't. (*Lights fade on his smile.*)

END OF ACT ONE

ACT TWO

Scene One

The same scene, late winter. A gloomy day. Early after-noon. Honeyman enters quickly, looking around. He wears a topcoat. Suddenly Botvinnik hurries on from the opposite direction. He seems to be chasing something—he looks here and there along the ground—ignoring Honeyman. Honeyman suddenly sees something in the woods and calls out.

HONEYMAN. That way! He's over there!

BOTVINNIK. (*Off.*) Where?!

HONEYMAN. There! By that log! (*Botvinnik rushes off in the direction Honeyman indicates.*) No—the other side! Right underneath!

BOTVINNIK. (*Off.*) You mean this . . . ? Oh—*damn! K chortu!*

HONEYMAN. What? Andrey?

BOTVINNIK. (*Off.*) He ran right by me! (*We hear more rustling. Botvinnik appears.*) He got away. (*A little out of breath.*) I am too old for this. I used to be able to catch them every time.

HONEYMAN. You did? Alone?

BOTVINNIK. Of course alone. You must catch a rabbit alone. Otherwise there is no challenge. If there was snow, I would have seen his tracks. I would have had him. (*Botvinnik winces, holds his side.*)

HONEYMAN. Are you all right?

BOTVINNIK. (*Sitting on the bench.*) It's nothing. A muscle. (*Suddenly taking note of Honeyman.*) I'm sorry. Did this surprise you?

HONEYMAN. A little.

BOTVINNIK. I always try to catch rabbits. I used to, any-way. When I was a boy.

HONEYMAN. You did? Why?

BOTVINNIK. It was fun. I was very fast once. Really. I chased them all the time. It became a . . . reflex, yes? Whenever I was out walking, if I saw a rabbit—whoosh! Into the woods. And today, to come here, to see a rabbit on the

33

bench—sitting here—I couldn't help myself. You understand.

HONEYMAN. Certainly.

BOTVINNIK. I caught a lot of them. When I was young. Finally I stopped.

HONEYMAN. Why?

BOTVINNIK. The war came. We couldn't leave Leningrad. I caught rats instead. For food. But that's the war, and you do not wish me to mention the war, so I am sorry and I shut up, yes? (*A beat.*) It's pretty out here, eh? This time of year. Away from that little room. Months and months in the same room. Negotiating.

HONEYMAN. Don't complain. You've had the last two weeks in Moscow.

BOTVINNIK. You think they don't have little rooms in Moscow? No, this is the best. To be outdoors. It improves concentration, I think. To get away. To sit quietly in the world.

HONEYMAN. How was Moscow?

BOTVINNIK. Hm?

HONEYMAN. Moscow. How was it? You had some fairly important meetings there. I thought you asked me out here so you could fill me in.

BOTVINNIK. (*A bit distracted.*) What? Oh, yes . . . yes . . . I did.

HONEYMAN. So?

BOTVINNIK. What?

HONEYMAN. Fill me in.

BOTVINNIK. You want to start right now?

HONEYMAN. Why not?

BOTVINNIK. It's just that it's so good to be here again. Among the trees. (*A beat. Botvinnik stares off.*)

HONEYMAN. Is anything wrong?

BOTVINNIK. Hm? No.

HONEYMAN. You seem a little distracted.

BOTVINNIK. (*Sharply.*) I am not. I am completely concentrated.

HONEYMAN. It's just that you seem . . .

BOTVINNIK. How I seem is not important. How I am is important, yes?

34

HONEYMAN. How are you?
BOTVINNIK. (*With sudden force, looking away from Honeyman.*) I should have caught that rabbit! (*A beat.*)
HONEYMAN. Andrey . . .
BOTVINNIK. When I was a boy, people were amazed at me. Amazed. So quick, they would say. He catches them with his bare hands. (*A beat. Honeyman studies Botvinnik. Botvinnik catches his stare, tries to return it, then looks away.*) When was the last time we were here?
HONEYMAN. A month ago.
BOTVINNIK. A month ago. What did we talk about?
HONEYMAN. Modifying negotiation procedures, Soviet-American relations and Babe Ruth.
BOTVINNIK. Ah! The Babe! The Sultan of Swat.
HONEYMAN. Andrey . . .
BOTVINNIK. Magnificent athlete. Larger than life.
HONEYMAN. Would you mind if we don't start with the frivolous side of things today?
BOTVINNIK. You don't want to?
HONEYMAN. No.
BOTVINNIK. Why not?
HONEYMAN. Because you have news for me. You've been in Moscow. You're back now. You have news. I want to hear it. (*A beat.*)
BOTVINNIK. What if it's not good news?
HONEYMAN. I want to hear it. (*A beat.*) Your government rejected our proposal, didn't they?
BOTVINNIK. Not exactly.
HONEYMAN. What do you mean?
BOTVINNIK. They didn't reject your proposal itself. They rejected what your President has turned the proposal into.
HONEYMAN. Which is?
BOTVINNIK. Which is — in their words — a cynical public relations scheme.
HONEYMAN. It is not a cynical . . .
BOTVINNIK. It is. From the moment he announced it to the world.
HONEYMAN. He had to announce it.
BOTVINNIK. Why? When we had not agreed to it yet.
HONEYMAN. You never agreed to anything! You accepted

one small point, before our election, and since then — nothing, zero, no movement all winter. He couldn't wait any longer.

BOTVINNIK. You should have stopped him.

HONEYMAN. I tried. I argued him out of going public on this three times in the past five months. You know that.

BOTVINNIK. You should have argued again.

HONEYMAN. I did. But I was running out of ammunition.

BOTVINNIK. So. In one speech he destroys all the work we have done. Good. Fine. Why not?

HONEYMAN. You were the ones who destroyed it. By delay.

BOTVINNIK. Delay does not destroy agreements. One can always renew efforts. But to announce the proposal . . .

HONEYMAN. He had the right.

BOTVINNIK. He bears the responsibility!

HONEYMAN. For what? For telling the world? Why's that so terrible?

BOTVINNIK. Don't be ridiculous.

HONEYMAN. No, tell me. Why is it so bad if the world knows what we're discussing?

BOTVINNIK. Because it makes us look like fools. If we accept your proposal now, what will the rest of the world say? "Ah, the Americans have finally thought of a clever plan. Thank God the unimaginative Russians have agreed."

HONEYMAN. The rest of the world, if they said anything, would say, "At last — two maniacs have had a moment of sanity."

BOTVINNIK. Yes, they would say that too, but first they would say it is an American peace, an American security.

HONEYMAN. Who cares whose peace it is?

BOTVINNIK. You do. You do not want a Russian peace. Two years ago we announced to the world a plan of our own — just as good as yours. And you rejected it.

HONEYMAN. There were significant problems with that plan.

BOTVINNIK. Yes, it was ours. Now please, John — stop pretending. You know neither of our countries can afford to be second in the quest for peace.

HONEYMAN. What quest for peace? At this rate there is no quest for peace.

BOTVINNIK. But there's the quest for the appearance of the quest for peace. These are negotiations, John. There are rules. There are forms. You know them as well as I do. Your President knows them, too. When he announced the proposal, he knew we would have to reject it. (*A beat. Honeyman expels a long sigh.*)

HONEYMAN. Why did your government delay so long? What was it about the proposal you objected to?

BOTVINNIK. Why go into it?

HONEYMAN. *It's our job.* (*A beat.*) Was it the total number of warheads?

BOTVINNIK. John . . .

HONEYMAN. Was it?

BOTVINNIK. No.

HONEYMAN. The percentage of land-based missiles?

BOTVINNIK. No.

HONEYMAN. Data exchange? On site inspections?

BOTVINNIK. It's useless to . . .

HONEYMAN. I want to know. Cruise missile reductions? Mobile missile verification?

BOTVINNIK. Not really.

HONEYMAN. The testing moratorium? The research question?

BOTVINNIK. No.

HONEYMAN. BMD restrictions? The ASAT provisions?

BOTVINNIK. It wasn't any . . .

HONEYMAN. C-cubed issues? SLBMs? MX?

BOTVINNIK. No! Not MX or SLBMs or SLCMs or SDI or FBS or CEP or SALT or START or any of it. We had no objections to anything in your proposal. You understand? Nothing. (*A beat.*)

HONEYMAN. Nothing?

BOTVINNIK. Nothing. We liked the whole proposal.

HONEYMAN. I don't understand. You liked it?

BOTVINNIK. Very much.

HONEYMAN. Then why did you delay so long?

BOTVINNIK. Because your proposal was . . . too good.

HONEYMAN. Too good?

BOTVINNIK. It could have led to real arms reductions. Serious ones.

HONEYMAN. Don't you want that?

BOTVINNIK. Of course. But . . . also we are afraid of it.

HONEYMAN. Why? It's a treaty. We've made treaties before.

BOTVINNIK. Look at those treaties, John. They aren't treaties — they're blueprints. We determine what weapons we'll build in the next few years, then agree to let each other build them. We get rid of small systems so that we can keep bigger ones. We trade obsolete technology for state-of-the-art, we take weapons out of Europe so we can put up new ones in space. Then we say to the world, "See? We are capable of restraint. Here is a small step forward." It is laughable.

HONEYMAN. But it is a step forward. Every treaty is. Each time we come — stumbling — to some sort of an agreement, even if it's self-serving, even if it's flawed . . . that's progress.

BOTVINNIK. It is not progress to take a step and slide back three. Every ten years we wake up and say, "It is time to take the first step." But meanwhile we have spent a decade creating bargaining chips — new weapons built expressly so they can be bargained away later. And what is the result? We build and get rid of bargaining chips. Nothing more. The real arsenals remain untouched. In fact, they grow.

HONEYMAN. You're right. Each year, each month, each day someone is proposing a new weapons system. Someone is securing a grant for more research, dreaming up a new technology that will do God-knows-what destruction — to our economies, if nothing else. How, knowing that, can we let any opportunity slip through our fingers? Especially this opportunity, this treaty, these comprehensive reductions. These *real* reductions.

BOTVINNIK. I know, I know. But we have problems with reductions such as these.

HONEYMAN. What are they?

BOTVINNIK. We don't trust you.

HONEYMAN. You don't trust us?

BOTVINNIK. Do you trust *us*?

HONEYMAN. Yes. Well—we try to. But whether we trust each other or not, the proposal has provisions. It has safeguards.

BOTVINNIK. We don't trust the safeguards.

HONEYMAN. There are checks on the safeguards. Verifications.

BOTVINNIK. We don't trust them.

HONEYMAN. Andrey . . .

BOTVINNIK. Even if there were checks on the checks on the checks, we wouldn't trust them.

HONEYMAN. Why not?

BOTVINNIK. Because we don't trust *you*. Who knows what you are making right now that lies outside this proposal?

HONEYMAN. We're not making any . . .

BOTVINNIK. Multiple warheads, Star Wars—these things came *after* treaties were signed, not before.

HONEYMAN. We can control new technologies. Together.

BOTVINNIK. Can we? How can you be sure of what's going on in your own country right now? Do you think they tell you everything? Face it, John—you can't even completely trust *your* side. And you want to trust ours?

HONEYMAN. We *can* work . . .

BOTVINNIK. Suppose we sign an agreement, and the next day you—or we—suddenly unveil a new weapon. What happens? Immediately, a new arms race.

HONEYMAN. Even if you're right—you're not, but even if you were . . .

BOTVINNIK. I am right. I am always right. And how do we appear to the rest of the world? As two warmongers who can't keep a treaty. If however, we have never agreed to a treaty, then when a new technology comes along, we are simply two nations who are trying to make a treaty, but who must remain prepared for war. It creates a much better impression.

HONEYMAN. Looking for peace, and purposely never finding it?

BOTVINNIK. (*Taking out his eyedrops, applying them.*) It is better for everyone. Broken treaties make people too nervous, yes?

HONEYMAN. So this makes your job and my job—what?

39

Sort of a nuclear night light? Providing no real hope, just . . .
BOTVINNIK. The appearance. Yes.
HONEYMAN. This is what you truly think is preferable?
BOTVINNIK. Not I. My leaders. Your leaders.
HONEYMAN. How long do you — do they — think this is supposed to go on?
BOTVINNIK. (*Shrugging, putting away his eyedrops.*) Until the world ends.
HONEYMAN. Which could be tomorrow. Andrey, it's no argument to say we can't negotiate because we don't trust each other. That should be just what spurs us on: the need to develop better systems of trust — to combat each new weapons system, in turn. For every new weapons system, a new *trust* system.
BOTVINNIK. I agree.
HONEYMAN. You do? Well, good. Then if we . . .
BOTVINNIK. The only problem is one of pace.
HONEYMAN. Pace? What do you mean?
BOTVINNIK. We are diplomats . . .
HONEYMAN. Negotiators.
BOTVINNIK. Negotiators. We work at a certain pace. We build trust. Genuine trust. It takes decades. In that time, weapons makers create two or three new waves of nuclear arms. Each new wave pushes us farther back. Who is ready to say, "Put these weapons on hold — Botvinnik and Honeyman *almost* trust each other"? Meanwhile, with each new wave, the warning time gets shorter. From an hour, to half an hour, twenty minutes, ten, five, four . . . finally to no warning at all. No chance to react. Missiles may fly over anytime. Who can stand the responsibility? In the end, we will not be consulted when war begins — not even our leaders will be. A computer will declare war on another computer — because the *computer* got nervous.
HONEYMAN. And you and I will die here? In mid-sentence?
BOTVINNIK. Right between the words "arms" and "control." It is not that you and I are failing to make progress. It's that those who build arms make so *much* progress.

HONEYMAN. There has to be a way to formulate an agreement that takes this into account.

BOTVINNIK. You want to take irrationality into account? Very good. I applaud this. But I warn you — no government has ever been rational, even about conventional weapons. You expect them to be rational about nuclear ones?

HONEYMAN. Governments can learn to be rational.

BOTVINNIK. Impossible. They are too irrational. All of them. *And* all of them are getting nuclear weapons. Once we only had to be rational in English and Russian. Now we must do it in Hebrew, Hindi, Afrikaans . . . These countries look to us to show the way — and what do we teach? Never go back. Never give up your nuclear threat. My friend, it is all irrationality.

HONEYMAN. It's not *all* irrationality . . .

BOTVINNIK. (*Cutting him off sharply.*) What do you know about it?! *I* have been here for years. I've seen how it works! (*An embarrassed pause. Honeyman stares at him.*)

HONEYMAN. You hate this more than I do, don't you?

BOTVINNIK. Of course not. It's not a matter of hate.

HONEYMAN. Sounded like hate to me.

BOTVINNIK. I gave up hate long ago. I now only study these things.

HONEYMAN. You study them pretty hard.

BOTVINNIK. I have much experience.

HONEYMAN. You have much anger — that's what you have.

BOTVINNIK. Anger is useless to a diplomat.

HONEYMAN. Then why do you feel it?

BOTVINNIK. I do *not* feel anger . . .

HONEYMAN. Sounded like anger . . .

BOTVINNIK. *This is not anger! This is careful study! Nothing more!* (*A beat.*)

HONEYMAN. I must be mistaken.

BOTVINNIK. Yes. You must.

HONEYMAN. Well. I won't accuse you anymore of being human.

BOTVINNIK. Thank you. It is now time to talk about something besides negotiations.

41

HONEYMAN. Are you sure? It's just that if we're both feeling this same . . . frustration, maybe we should find a way to . . .

BOTVINNIK. When two men are dying of cancer, what do they discuss? Cancer? No. It's bad taste. They talk about something else.

HONEYMAN. Andrey, we have a function here.

BOTVINNIK. *Yes, and now you know what it is!* (*A beat.*) It is not always pleasant to discover what you were meant for. (*Botvinnik moves away from him.*)

HONEYMAN. I'm sorry.

BOTVINNIK. Sorry? For what? For baiting me? It's your job. I'm glad to see you're finally getting the hang of it. (*A silence. Botvinnik stares off into the distance, Honeyman sits on the bench, pondering. When he speaks, his tone is thoughtful.*)

HONEYMAN. I think the answer lies in . . . resisting. Resisting irrationality.

BOTVINNIK. No one can do that. The fear is too great. The temptation is too great.

HONEYMAN. I did it. (*Botvinnik regards him skeptically.*) I did. Before coming here. They sent me on a tour. An overview, really. You know, spend a little time with the military, get a sense of how much we've invested, look over the hardware — hopefully fall in love with it.

BOTVINNIK. And did you?

HONEYMAN. I was touring ICBM sites in North Dakota. Just riding around, staring down into holes all day at these huge, shiny . . . perfect things. These missiles.

BOTVINNIK. And you fell in love?

HONEYMAN. On our way back, we stopped for gas. We were in a small town called Rugby — and right there next to the highway was a little stone monument. It marked the exact geographical center of North America. The whole damn continent. This was the center.

BOTVINNIK. Is it a significant place?

HONEYMAN. It's meaningless. It's just endless, flat landscape. But we had put all these missiles there. Right in the dead, blank heart of the continent. In the center. In an emptiness. In our emptiness. (*A beat.*) And I liked it. It filled something up. I wanted there to be more missiles.

BOTVINNIK. You are a very honest man.

HONEYMAN. But I *thought* about it. I thought about it until I knew I could not afford that feeling. Ever again, in my life.

BOTVINNIK. And what about honesty?

HONEYMAN. Is it honest for an addict to use a drug, just because he wants it? Is it honest for us to have missiles because on some level we want missiles? No. We resist. We reason ourselves out of it.

BOTVINNIK. Just as the addict "reasons" himself out of the drug?

HONEYMAN. It can be done.

BOTVINNIK. (*Without conviction.*) Certainly.

HONEYMAN. I've done it. You've done it.

BOTVINNIK. Perhaps. But who's listening to us? No, the sad fact is, you and I are meant for nothing more than playing games in the woods.

HONEYMAN. We are not meant for playing games in the woods.

BOTVINNIK. We are. Thank goodness we are friends, yes? Or it would be intolerable.

HONEYMAN. It *is* intolerable. And we're not friends. My God, this isn't a friendship. How can two people who have nothing to do be friends? They can't even be people! I thought, when I came here, I was going to have some influence—that what I said or did was going to affect *some*body, *some*place. But obviously that's not the case. Obviously I'm not here at all, right? And if *I'm* not here, God knows where you are. You've been a nonentity a lot longer than me. You've got the act down pat. You don't want a friend, you want someone to be dead with! (*A beat.*) I wish, at least, that you had fought for this proposal.

BOTVINNIK. I fought.

HONEYMAN. I can imagine.

BOTVINNIK. I *fought.* Even though I knew they would not accept it. Even though it was dangerous. I fought anyway.

HONEYMAN. Oh you did, did you? Why?

BOTVINNIK. *Because I like you.* Whether I am dead or not. (*A beat.*) Besides, it was a good proposal. I will miss it. (*A beat.*)

HONEYMAN. There's something I'd like you to look over.

BOTVINNIK. What is it? (*Honeyman reaches into his coat*

pocket and produces a folded piece of paper.)

HONEYMAN. The proposal. The very same proposal, with a few cosmetic changes, that's all.

BOTVINNIK. So?

HONEYMAN. What if I can get the President to offer it again? Secretly. The same plan for an agreement — only with a new name, a few insignificant points altered to save face for both countries. Would your side be interested in that?

BOTVINNIK. Who told you to do this?

HONEYMAN. No one. It's my own idea.

BOTVINNIK. We can get in trouble for this.

HONEYMAN. I don't care. Do you?

BOTVINNIK. You never give up, do you? (*Botvinnik takes the paper, regards it, then points at something in it.*) This is not an insignificant point.

HONEYMAN. (*Looking.*) What? Of course it is.

BOTVINNIK. I do not think it is insignificant.

HONEYMAN. Well, fine. Change it back then. The point is . . .

BOTVINNIK. I don't have a pen. (*Honeyman furnishes him with a rather expensive-looking pen.*)

HONEYMAN. (*As Botvinnik makes occasional changes in the document.*) The point is, we may still be able to salvage this plan. After all, what are we — facilitators, right? Our whole job is to help two giants come to grips with each other. If we can just . . . (*Growing more nervous at the number of changes Botvinnik is making.*) What are you changing now?

BOTVINNIK. You'll see.

HONEYMAN. If we can just hold these ideas together, we might make some progress here. If I can get this to the President directly, before Defense and State pull their usual . . . Are you through?

BOTVINNIK. Almost. (*He finishes, starts to give the pen back, stops, looks at it.*) Japanese. Very nice. (*He gives the pen to Honeyman, regards the paper again. Honeyman controls his eagerness to look at it.*) Do you want to see? (*Honeyman quickly grabs the paper.*)

HONEYMAN. (*Nodding as he reads.*) OK . . . OK . . . That one's OK . . .

44

BOTVINNIK. Only OK? I think it's very nice.
HONEYMAN. It's OK. It was better before.
BOTVINNIK. Oh no, no, it was . . . (*Honeyman holds up a hand. Botvinnik falls silent. Honeyman finishes, thinks a long moment. Botvinnik's curiosity grows.*) What do you think?
HONEYMAN. (*After a pause as much to himself as Botvinnik.*) This would be all right. I think I could get the President's approval for this. Will you take it to your side?
BOTVINNIK. As your proposal?
HONEYMAN. As anyone's proposal. As nobody's proposal.
BOTVINNIK. But here it is. A paper, in our hands.
HONEYMAN. A non-paper. No addresses, no signatures . . . just something that's there . . . for both sides to examine. Privately.
BOTVINNIK. I'm walking on eggs just now, at home.
HONEYMAN. I realize that.
BOTVINNIK. They think I've been awfully . . . active, this year. (*A beat. Botvinnik thinks.*) But I could try.
HONEYMAN. Thank you. Well, we should get back, huh? (*Botvinnik remains seated, holding the paper.*)
BOTVINNIK. Things have not gone smoothly for this proposal.
HONEYMAN. We should get this into both languages before . . .
BOTVINNIK. We've had a difficult time of it, haven't we? Over this.
HONEYMAN. Pretty difficult, yes. Come on, we can still . . .
BOTVINNIK. I'm glad it's been difficult. It allows you to feel something.
HONEYMAN. What?
BOTVINNIK. The disappointment. (*Rising.*) I think my leaders may accept this now.
HONEYMAN. Good. That would be wonderful.
BOTVINNIK. I think perhaps your side will reject it.
HONEYMAN. Our own plan?
BOTVINNIK. *Nobody's* plan.
HONEYMAN. Why should we?
BOTVINNIK. You want rationality . . . ? You and I only make recommendations. Our leaders must make decisions.

Perhaps some decisions are too big to make.

HONEYMAN. Someone has to make them.

BOTVINNIK. Maybe you are right. Maybe your President will embrace this plan. All things are possible while we are still alive, yes?

HONEYMAN. He will embrace it. I'll convince him.

BOTVINNIK. Of course.

HONEYMAN. You'll see. I think you'll be very surprised this time, Andrey. Very surprised indeed. I *can* convince him.

BOTVINNIK. (*Holding the paper out to him.*) Hope is a true miracle, is it not? (*Honeyman takes the paper.*)

HONEYMAN. So is trust.

BOTVINNIK. Well, it's time to go back. It's getting cold.

HONEYMAN. Really? I hadn't noticed.

BOTVINNIK. (*Smiling.*) Indeed. Come. It's important to go back together today.

HONEYMAN. Why?

BOTVINNIK. Because we don't often do that, and they will be confused. (*They exit together. Lights fade to black.*)

END OF ACT TWO, SCENE ONE

SCENE TWO

The same scene. Six weeks later—early spring. The woods are filled with warm, late-afternoon light. Spring flowers cover the area. Honeyman sits on the bench, staring straight ahead. Botvinnik is Upstage, bent over, picking flowers at the edge of the trees.

BOTVINNIK. This will be the last one. This will be the final, glorious touch, eh? (*He straightens up, reveals a small bouquet of fresh-picked wildflowers.*) It needed a little blue, don't you think?

HONEYMAN. (*Without looking.*) I suppose.

BOTVINNIK. What is this flower called? This blue one?

HONEYMAN. It's called a flower.

BOTVINNIK. No, no, no—what would a botanist call it?

(*Botvinnik places the bouquet in Honeyman's lap. Honeyman looks down at it.*)

HONEYMAN. A flower.

BOTVINNIK. No. If he had to designate it. For another scientist.

HONEYMAN. A flower. (*A beat. Botvinnik moves to look at the woods.*)

BOTVINNIK. The woods are filled with them. It's very beautiful this time of year. Don't you think?

HONEYMAN. Aren't you even a little bit angry? (*Botvinnik smiles.*)

BOTVINNIK. I remember the first time my leaders said no to an agreement I had worked out. It was with Mr. McIntyre's predecessor, Mr. . . .

HONEYMAN. Mr. Sand.

BOTVINNIK. Yes. Mr. Sand. He and I worked a very long time on that one. We had such . . . large dreams. We were both new. Each of us was so eager, so . . . overjoyed at the creativity of our solutions. We marched out of this very woods and told the world. "A major arms reduction," we said, "A path to sanity." Of course, four weeks later our governments politely suggested we had overstepped our authority. "Go back to the table, work a little more," they said. "And stay out of the woods." (*A beat.*) This proposal didn't do so badly. At least it was six weeks before your President . . .

HONEYMAN. (*More to himself than Botvinnik.*) He looked me straight in the eye and said, "Don't try so hard." Don't *try* so hard. (*Honeyman throws the flowers to the ground.*)

BOTVINNIK. It was only a euphemism.

HONEYMAN. For what?

BOTVINNIK. For don't try at all. (*Botvinnik bends to pick up the flowers.*) Really, you must control yourself. Switzerland has strict laws about littering.

HONEYMAN. I know.

BOTVINNIK. They are terribly compulsive about it. It can be quite risky to throw things . . .

HONEYMAN. I *know.* I was almost arrested for it this morning.

BOTVINNIK. You were? Really? Tell me about it.

47

HONEYMAN. I don't want to talk about it. It's a pointless story.

BOTVINNIK. Oh, please—tell me. An arrest in Switzerland. How wonderful.

HONEYMAN. It was nothing. I threw a gum wrapper on the sidewalk. (*Botvinnik gasps in mock horror.*) Really, there are more important things to talk about.

BOTVINNIK. Not today. (*Honeyman looks away from him.*) Please. Let's take advantage of this exquisite time when everything has broken down. Tell me your pointless story.

HONEYMAN. Why?

BOTVINNIK. It will be such a relief.

HONEYMAN. For who?

BOTVINNIK. For you. (*A beat.*)

HONEYMAN. It was nothing. I threw this wrapper, and suddenly there was this very old man beside me, grabbing me. I thought he was a lunatic—he was yelling at me in German. Why did he yell in German? Do I dress like a German? (*Botvinnik shrugs.*) He was trying to make me stop. I speeded up—I didn't know who he was.

BOTVINNIK. He could have been a very old terrorist.

HONEYMAN. Why am I telling this?

BOTVINNIK. Because it is crucial. Go on.

HONEYMAN. He yelled at me louder—in French this time. I stopped and stared at him. I didn't say anything, I just stared. He kept right on yelling, only he switched to Italian. This went on for a solid minute—like I was his bad child—*all* in Italian. Finally I broke in. I said, "I don't speak Italian," and he went back to French.

BOTVINNIK. No.

HONEYMAN. Yes! I said, "I don't speak French," and he went back to German.

BOTVINNIK. Really?

HONEYMAN. Yes! So I yelled back at him: "I don't speak French, German or Italian! I'm an American, damn it! What the hell do you want?!" And he turned and pointed at my gum wrapper. And then I saw he was a cop. He was a Swiss policeman.

BOTVINNIK. Oh, dear.

48

HONEYMAN. I didn't notice at first. He had his hat in his hand, and he was so . . . old, that I . . . But there he was, in a uniform. He must've been going to his own retirement party.

BOTVINNIK. Swiss police are very officious.

HONEYMAN. And he tried to drag me back to this gum wrapper. He literally tried to drag me. I said, "Tell me what you want." And he said, "*Aufheben!*" The paper. "*Aufheben!*"

BOTVINNIK. Pick it up.

HONEYMAN. Exactly.

BOTVINNIK. And did you?

HONEYMAN. No, I didn't pick it up.

BOTVINNIK. Really? Why not?

HONEYMAN. Would *you?*

BOTVINNIK. Of course.

HONEYMAN. You'd let a little old man drag you back? A little old Swiss . . . joke of a policeman? With people watching?

BOTVINNIK. Especially with people watching.

HONEYMAN. Well, I didn't. I pulled my arm away. I wanted to say, "Look — I spend all day, every day, working to prevent the total destruction of every living thing on this planet. The whole planet. Even Switzerland. I'm trying to preserve the last few precious days of life you may have coming to you. But I can't do it if I'm not allowed to throw gum wrappers on the sidewalk. Do you understand? It's too much pressure! I can't worry about everything!"

BOTVINNIK. But you didn't say that.

HONEYMAN. No. I said, "I'm a very important person."

BOTVINNIK. What did he say to you?

HONEYMAN. "*Aufheben!*"

BOTVINNIK. And you said?

HONEYMAN. No! Then he tried to arrest me. He flashed his pitiful Swiss badge and put his hat on. By this time old people were stopping, looking at me and shaking their heads. As though the wrapper was a . . . dead infant or something. A couple of teenagers were standing there, laughing.

BOTVINNIK. Congratulations! An international incident!

HONEYMAN. Anyway, he tried to grab me again, and

I . . . I don't know why I did this, but I ac-
tually . . . pushed him.
BOTVINNIK. No.
HONEYMAN. I don't know why I did it.
BOTVINNIK. Did you hurt him?
HONEYMAN. No, he didn't even fall over. But the others
—the people around us—they gasped. They literally
gasped. The old cop stared at me like I was insane.
BOTVINNIK. You were.
HONEYMAN. So I quick pulled out my identification and
held it open and said, "Diplomat." And pointed to myself.
And the cop just . . . shrank . . . from me. I took a step
toward him and said, "Diplomat" again, and he just kept
backing away. And the whole crowd backed away. I kept
saying, "It's all right—I'm a diplomat," but the circle of
people got wider and wider, and the cop turned and walked
away from me as fast as he could. And everyone else did the
same. Except the two teenagers. They just stared at me. Not
like they expected me to do anything. Just . . . because I
was the only thing left to look at. (*A beat.*) I've never behaved
that way in public before.
BOTVINNIK. You were having a bad day.
HONEYMAN. I was not having a bad day! I was . . . I am
turning into something here. Some kind of monster. Some
kind of littering, old-man-pushing, diplomatic . . . mon-
ster. Some special, newly-created kind of . . . *thing.* (*A beat.
Quietly.*) What are we doing here?
BOTVINNIK. We are talking.
HONEYMAN. No, I mean—what on Earth . . . are we
doing?
BOTVINNIK. The questions you ask are too large. Let me
ask a smaller one. What is your favorite color?
HONEYMAN. My favorite color?
BOTVINNIK. Yes. What is it?
HONEYMAN. Why do you want to know that?
BOTVINNIK. I have my reasons. Is it green? Red? Yellow?
HONEYMAN. I don't want to talk about this.
BOTVINNIK. It's a simple question. I'm sure we can handle
it.
HONEYMAN. Don't mock me!

BOTVINNIK. You're offended.

HONEYMAN. Yes, I'm offended, I'm disgusted, I'm
. . . *What are we doing here?!*

BOTVINNIK. My favorite color is blue.

HONEYMAN. Stop talking about colors!!

BOTVINNIK. I have to talk about colors.

HONEYMAN. Why!?

BOTVINNIK. I want to buy you a gift.

HONEYMAN. We give each other gifts all the time. That's
what international negotiating teams do: sit down, stare at
each other for a few months, exchange gifts and leave. (*With
a look at Botvinnik.*) Why does your delegation want to give us
gifts?

BOTVINNIK. No, no. Not our delegation. Just me. *I* want
to give *you* a gift. A tie, perhaps. In a color you like. Something you will be happy to have.

HONEYMAN. Why?

BOTVINNIK. Do I need a reason?

HONEYMAN. Yes.

BOTVINNIK. As a consolation prize, then. Because we will
never achieve a treaty.

HONEYMAN. We will achieve a treaty. Someday we will.

BOTVINNIK. Very well, then — a victory prize. I want to
give you a gift. What does it matter why?

HONEYMAN. It could be the difference between honoring
me and humiliating me.

BOTVINNIK. What about blue? (*Honeyman sighs.*) Is blue
your favorite?

HONEYMAN. No, it's not.

BOTVINNIK. Brown?

HONEYMAN. Nobody's favorite color is brown.

BOTVINNIK. Why do you make me guess? Tell me.

HONEYMAN. My favorite color is orange.

BOTVINNIK. Orange?

HONEYMAN. Yes. Orange.

BOTVINNIK. You expect me to buy you an orange tie?

HONEYMAN. Don't buy me a tie! I don't want a tie!

BOTVINNIK. All right, I won't.

HONEYMAN. Good! I can see why McIntyre left.

BOTVINNIK. You think he left because of me.

HONEYMAN. Who wouldn't? No one can deal with you. You take serious things lightly, light things seriously, you waste months of time — and what's worse, you never even *try* to be optimistic. Don't you see how killing that is?

BOTVINNIK. No.

HONEYMAN. How can you be so negative?

BOTVINNIK. You're the one who doesn't want a tie.

HONEYMAN. I think you were made for this place. You were born to sit and stare at the world and say no.

BOTVINNIK. Why, because I am Russian?

HONEYMAN. Not because you're . . .

BOTVINNIK. That's it, isn't it? You think Russians are all alike. You think we train our children to say no at the dinner table. "Do you want your food?" "No!" "Something to drink?" "No!"

HONEYMAN. Andrey . . .

BOTVINNIK. You think we like to say no. You think we train our backsides to sit for days without pain, yes?

HONEYMAN. (*Rising.*) I'm going back now, Andrey.

BOTVINNIK. No!

HONEYMAN. Why not!?

BOTVINNIK. I have something to tell you.

HONEYMAN. What?

BOTVINNIK. Guess.

HONEYMAN. No!

BOTVINNIK. You are so negative. Very well, I will tell you. I'm leaving. (*A beat.*)

HONEYMAN. What?

BOTVINNIK. I'm leaving. Bye-bye.

HONEYMAN. You mean, you're going back home for a week or two . . . ?

BOTVINNIK. No, I'm leaving.

HONEYMAN. (*Alarmed.*) Your government's pulling out the delegation?

BOTVINNIK. No, no — listen to your language, John. They're staying. I — Andrey Lvovich Botvinnik — *I* am leaving. For good. Good-bye. (*Botvinnik extends his hand.*)

HONEYMAN. (*Not taking it.*) You're leaving your post?

BOTVINNIK. Yes.

HONEYMAN. Why? We're in the middle of negotiations.

52

BOTVINNIK. I will be replaced. (*A beat.*)

HONEYMAN. When are you leaving?

BOTVINNIK. A week or two.

HONEYMAN. A week . . . ! How soon'll you be replaced?

BOTVINNIK. A month or two.

HONEYMAN. Andrey . . . !

BOTVINNIK. Are you worried about delay? That is your job, delay. In all my years here it has been one, long delay. So tell me — do you have a favorite color besides orange? I would like to get you something.

HONEYMAN. A farewell gift?

BOTVINNIK. Yes. (*A beat.*)

HONEYMAN. Are they making you retire?

BOTVINNIK. Of course not.

HONEYMAN. Is it because you pushed for our proposal? Did you get in trouble with . . .

BOTVINNIK. You Americans always think the same thing. Kremlin intrigue. Trips to Siberia. No, I merely intend to go home. It is time.

HONEYMAN. Is it a medical problem?

BOTVINNIK. No.

HONEYMAN. It's just that you've seemed more . . . distracted than usual. In the sessions.

BOTVINNIK. Me? What about you? Pushing old men in the street.

HONEYMAN. That was . . .

BOTVINNIK. You don't have to apologize. No — I have served for many years here by doing absolutely nothing. Now it is time for a new man to come and do absolutely nothing. In this way we achieve continuity of results. (*Holds his hand out to shake again.*) So. It has been very pleasurable with you. I thank you and say good-bye.

HONEYMAN. (*Not taking his hand.*) Why are you leaving?

BOTVINNIK. I told you. Shake.

HONEYMAN. Why are you leaving?

BOTVINNIK. There is no real reason. I am losing . . . concentration at the table — a little bit. My mind is beginning to wander . . . slightly . . . when I am there.

HONEYMAN. To wander?

BOTVINNIK. More and more. (*A beat.*)

HONEYMAN. Why not take some time off? A week or two? Maybe that would . . .

BOTVINNIK. That would do nothing. I am degenerating. It happens to everyone. Each day now I feel like I could say . . . anything. The worst thing. At the worst moment. It is an interesting feeling. It's like my brain is drying up, instead of my eyes. Work without hope is a dry thing. It is better, more realistic. But it is very dry. Will you miss me?

HONEYMAN. Don't go.

BOTVINNIK. I have to.

HONEYMAN. Rest a little. You can come back.

BOTVINNIK. The decay is inevitable.

HONEYMAN. It's not inevitable. Don't go. We're working on something here, Andrey.

BOTVINNIK. On what?

HONEYMAN. On *something*. My God — we've established a process, the two of us. If you're replaced, that's all gone.

BOTVINNIK. No, it isn't. The new man will . . .

HONEYMAN. The new man will not be you. (*A beat.*)

BOTVINNIK. You're very flattering. But let me make a suggestion. If you are so unhappy that I am leaving, then why don't you leave too?

HONEYMAN. Don't be ridiculous.

BOTVINNIK. It's not ridiculous. I go back to Leningrad, you go back to Vah-sow. We are both better off.

HONEYMAN. In what way?

BOTVINNIK. In every way. Listen to me — you're a good negotiator. You're smart, tough, charming. You can say no almost as well as me. They will keep you here a long time. And after long enough, you will be like I am now.

HONEYMAN. You're fine now.

BOTVINNIK. I don't even remember why I'm here. Leave when I do. Otherwise you will break down.

HONEYMAN. I won't.

BOTVINNIK. This morning you were almost arrested.

HONEYMAN. That was a freak accident.

BOTVINNIK. You will have more of them.

HONEYMAN. What if I do? What's it matter, as long as I'm here, working?

BOTVINNIK. Working for what? For progress? There is no progress here. Only the illusion. Every treaty we negotiated has been followed by an unprecedented arms buildup. Twenty-five years ago, we signed our first treaty. We had a few hundred warheads each. A few hundred. Today — thirteen treaties later — how many warheads do we have? Fifty thousand. If our leaders ever do accept real cuts, it will only be to gain a political advantage. When the advantage disappears, the cuts will too. There will be new weapons building. There will always be new weapons building. (*A beat.*) So listen to me: you are still young. Why grow old in this way?

HONEYMAN. Why should you care? You're leaving.

BOTVINNIK. I'm still your friend.

HONEYMAN. *Friends share hope*! If you go home now, we will never have been friends. Do you understand? We will have been colleagues, associates, counterparts, fellow workers on the same problem. Representatives, delegates, instruments of policy — but never — *never* — friends.

BOTVINNIK. (*Softly.*) I am *your* friend.

HONEYMAN. *Why*!? What do I do for you that makes you feel like a friend to me? What? Is it that we do the same thing? Have the same job?

BOTVINNIK. Of course not . . .

HONEYMAN. Then what? I don't think it's that we tell the same jokes. I don't think I tell any jokes at all, do I? I think I'm a pretty serious, stiff, even priggish type of person, wouldn't you say?

BOTVINNIK. At times.

HONEYMAN. All the time! And yet you like me. You want to be my friend. Why is that, Andrey? Do you want to get something from me? A bargaining advantage perhaps?

BOTVINNIK. Of course not . . .

HONEYMAN. You're damn right, of course not — you don't even remember why you're here. So what is it? What's the force that impels us towards each other? What is it we recognize in each other that makes us want to be friends? What is our special handicap as negotiators?

BOTVINNIK. (*Quietly.*) A conscience.

HONEYMAN. A conscience. Exactly. (*A beat.*) Do you think

the next two men in here will have a conscience? (*A beat.*)

BOTVINNIK. I can't stay. The process of replacing me has already begun. (*A silence.*) What will you do?

HONEYMAN. Stay. Work with your replacement. Hope for progress, for good faith, for enough time. Hope that hope itself isn't some . . . limitless desert we're all trying to cross.

BOTVINNIK. And if it is?

HONEYMAN. I'll die of hope.

BOTVINNIK. I will always like you. You will always be my favorite.

HONEYMAN. (*Simply.*) So what?

BOTVINNIK. Perhaps it is time to go.

HONEYMAN. Perhaps.

BOTVINNIK. (*Without moving.*) So — we are going. I am very serious about the tie, you know. What do you say to red?

HONEYMAN. I don't want a tie.

BOTVINNIK. Red is too political. Yellow? No, that stands for cowards, and you are too brave for your own good.

HONEYMAN. Andrey . . .

BOTVINNIK. Blue? No, blue is my favorite. It would be like forcing it on you . . .

HONEYMAN. *NO TIE! DO YOU HEAR ME?!! NO DAMN TIE! IF YOU EVER TRY TO GIVE ME A TIE, I'LL STUFF IT DOWN YOUR GODDAMN, FUCKING COMMUNIST THROAT!* (*A beat.*) I'm sorry.

BOTVINNIK. That is all right.

HONEYMAN. Sorry about "communist."

BOTVINNIK. No problem.

HONEYMAN. You're probably right. I'm probably crazy already.

BOTVINNIK. Probably.

HONEYMAN. But I'm staying. *I* have hope.

BOTVINNIK. You are entitled. Do you feel all right?

HONEYMAN. I'm fine.

BOTVINNIK. Shall we sit for awhile? (*Honeyman moves to the bench, sits. Botvinnik sits next to him. They are silent for a moment.*) This is very nice. Sitting here in nature. I can see why you like this. (*Honeyman looks at Botvinnik with surprise, then out at the woods.*)

HONEYMAN. When I was young, I used to think if you ate a lot of wild things — you know, if you went to the woods and gathered things: blueberries, mushrooms, asparagus — I thought eating those things would somehow make you . . . wild. Not wild-behaving, just more a part of that world. I mean, you'd be in a woods and feel completely comfortable there. You'd be at home. (*They stare at the woods.*)

BOTVINNIK. All these trees. One by one they will be chopped down, I think. And made into negotiating tables. The talks will go on for hundreds of years. If we are lucky. (*A beat.*) Our time together, John, has been a very great failure. (*Honeyman nods.*) But — a successful one. (*A beat.*) Shall we go back?

HONEYMAN. Let's stay awhile.

BOTVINNIK. Really? Do you want to? What do you want to talk about?

HONEYMAN. Nothing. (*Botvinnik regards him, then looks into the woods and nods. Honeyman stares into the distance as well. Botvinnik takes out his eyedrops and carefully applies them. Lights fade to black.*)

THE END

PROPERTY LIST

Act One — Scene 1

On Stage
Wooden bench

Personal
Eyedrops, with small plastic eyedropper ⎫ (Botvinnik)
Stone, in shoe ⎭

Act One — Scene 2

On Stage
Fallen leaves

Act Two — Scene 1

Personal
Expensive-looking pen   (Honeyman)
Folded paper   (Botvinnik)

Act Two — Scene 2

On Stage
Wildflowers

NEW
PLAYS

THE AFRICAN COMPANY PRESENTS
RICHARD III
by Carlyle Brown

EDWARD ALBEE'S
FRAGMENTS and THE MARRIAGE PLAY

IMAGINARY LIFE
by Peter Parnell

MIXED EMOTIONS
by Richard Baer

THE SWAN
by Elizabeth Egloff

Write for information as to availability
DRAMATISTS PLAY SERVICE, Inc.
440 Park Avenue South　　New York, N.Y. 10016

NEW
PLAYS

THE LIGHTS
by Howard Korder

THE TRIUMPH OF LOVE
by James Magruder

LATER LIFE
by A.R. Gurney

THE LOMAN FAMILY PICNIC
by Donald Margulies

A PERFECT GANESH
by Terrence McNally

SPAIN
by Romulus Linney

Write for information as to
availability
DRAMATISTS PLAY SERVICE, Inc.
440 Park Avenue South   New York, N.Y. 10016

NEW
PLAYS

LONELY PLANET
by Steven Dietz

THE AMERICA PLAY
by Suzan-Lori Parks

THE FOURTH WALL
by A.R. Gurney

JULIE JOHNSON
by Wendy Hammond

FOUR DOGS AND A BONE
by John Patrick Shanley

DESDEMONA, A PLAY ABOUT A HANDKERCHIEF
by Paula Vogel

Write for information as to availability
DRAMATISTS PLAY SERVICE, Inc.
440 Park Avenue South   New York, N.Y. 10016